A Very Special Sister

Dorothy Hoffman Levi ◆ Illustrations by Ethel Gold

Kendall Green Publications
Gallaudet University Press
Washington, D.C.

Kendall Green Publications
An imprint of Gallaudet University Press
800 Florida Avenue, N.E.
Washington, DC 20002-3695

Text ©1992 by Dorothy Hoffman Levi
Illustrations ©1992 by Ethel Gold
Printed in Singapore

Library of Congress Cataloging-in-Publication Data
Levi, Dorothy Hoffman, 1942-
    A very special sister/Dorothy Hoffman Levi: illustrations by
Ethel Gold.
      p. cm.
      Summary: Laura, who is deaf, is excited about becoming a big sister,
but she worries that a new baby who can hear might get more love from their
mother than she does. Text and illustrations provide instructions for signing
eight words.
   ISBN 0-930323-96-3
   [1. Deaf—Fiction.   2. Physically handicapped—Fiction.
3. Babies—Fiction.   4. Brothers and sisters—Fiction.]   I. Gold,
Ethel, ill.   II. Title.
PZ7.L5756Vf   1992
[E]—dc20
                                    91-25261
                                       CIP
                                       AC

For my parents, Ethel and Sid Hoffman, who nurtured the garden where love, compassion, and creativity always flourished. ◼

Laura did not like to keep secrets
from her best friend Frannie.

They talked to each other in two languages. Laura was deaf
and she taught Frannie how to sign. Frannie helped Laura
to say words clearly. Laura could read words on people's lips,
too. Frannie and Laura always told each other *everything*.

But one morning when the two girls walked to school, Laura looked as though she had a wonderful secret. Her eyes glowed like blue diamonds and her smile was as bright as a candle on a birthday cake.

"Why are you so happy today?" Frannie asked her.
"One of my wishes is coming true," Laura said.
"Really?" Frannie was surprised. "Which one?"
"I am going to be a big sister," Laura replied.
Frannie was so excited that she
hugged Laura and spun her
around and around.

When Jimmy, one of the boys in their class, saw them he wondered why the two girls were so happy. After he heard the good news, he asked Laura, "Do you think the baby will be a boy or a girl?"

"I don't know," she answered.

"Do you want a brother or a sister?" Jimmy asked.

"A sister, I think," Laura said.

"Why?" Jimmy sounded disappointed.

"Because girls are nice," Laura and Frannie answered at exactly the same time.

"Boys are nice, too," Jimmy said. "Do you want to know what boys are really like?"

When Laura and Frannie nodded, he said proudly, "Boys ride bicycles. They play ball. They hate to take baths."

Laura and Frannie looked at each other and then they began to laugh. "Girls ride bicycles. Girls play ball. And girls hate to take baths, too," Laura told him, signing as she spoke.

APRIL

SUNDAY	MONDAY	TUESDAY	WEDNESDAY	THURSDAY	FRIDAY	SATURDAY
		X	X 2	X 3	4	5
6	7	8	9	10	11	12
13	14	15	16	17	18	19
20	21	22	23	24	25	26
27	28	29	30			

Laura was glad that she had shared her secret with Frannie and Jimmy. The three children began to count the months, weeks, and days until the baby would arrive. Laura marked off the days on her calendar with a big red crayon. The baby would arrive in the summertime.

Laura was happy that the new baby was going to sleep in the room next to hers. She and her mother worked to get the room ready. Together, they painted the room bright yellow and put a border of nursery-rhyme characters around the top. They painted Laura's old crib and dresser sparkling white and fixed all her old toys so they looked like new. Even Laura's kitten Whiskers helped. Then, they bought new baby clothes that were so small they fit Laura's favorite doll.

By the end of school, Laura's mother was so big that she looked like a balloon about to burst. When Laura felt the baby kick inside her mother, she was very excited.

One afternoon Frannie came to visit. She asked Laura, "Will the baby be able to hear like I do?"

"I don't know," Laura answered. "Maybe she will not hear, like me."

That night Laura couldn't sleep. She wondered whether or not the new baby would be able to hear.

After that, Laura's big smile disappeared. She didn't ask her mother any more questions about the baby. She played alone, not with Frannie and Jimmy.

One summer day Laura's mother took Laura to the zoo. They watched the mother elephant playing with her new baby. They watched the baby monkeys having fun together.

They also saw mothers in the park wheeling baby carriages.
One of the babies smiled at Laura and reached out to touch her.
But she moved far away.

"Why are you sad, Laura?" her mother asked.

Laura didn't answer.

"Aren't you happy about our new baby?" her mother wondered.

Then Laura began to cry. "The baby will be able to hear," she said. "I can't hear. I'm afraid that you will love the new baby more than me."

"I can never love anyone more than I love you," Laura's mother said, holding her close.

"Really?" Laura asked. "But the new baby will hear your voice and I never can."

"You do hear my voice. Always, Laura," her mother said. "You hear my voice in your heart."

Laura smiled and hugged her mother. Just then the baby kicked hard. Laura and her mother laughed.

And the very next day, Laura was a big sister.

"Is the new baby a girl?" Frannie asked.

"Is the new baby a boy?" Jimmy asked.

"Both," Laura replied. "My mother had twins. One baby is a girl and one is a boy. I am a *double* big sister now."

"Can I help you take care of the babies?" Frannie asked.
"Yes," answered Laura, her eyes glowing.
"Can I help, too?" Jimmy wondered.
"Of course," said Laura with a big smile.

The twins could hear. They could hear Frannie and Jimmy. They could also hear Laura when she spoke and see her when she signed. And Laura could always hear the twins in her heart. She was a very special sister.

Some Signs You Can Learn

The directions for forming the signs are written and illustrated for right-handed people. If you are left-handed, substitute *left* wherever the directions say *right*. For example: to make the sign for *happy,* pat your chest with your right hand several times using upward movements. If you are left-handed, use your left hand. ▪

American Manual Alphabet

A   B   C   D   E   F   G

H   I   J   K   L   M

N   O   P   Q   R   S   T

U   V   W   X   Y   Z

happy
Pat your chest with your right hand several times using upward movements.

sister
Make an L handshape with your left hand and touch your right cheek with your right thumb. Bring your right hand down, changing to an L handshape, and place your right wrist on your left wrist, keeping both hands in L shape.

girl

Touch your cheek with your right thumb and move it toward your chin.

boy

Place your right hand above your right eye. Move thumb and fingertips together two times.

baby

Place your right lower arm inside your left lower arm and rock your arms back and forth.

heart

Use both middle fingers to draw a heart on the left side of your chest.

mother

Tap the thumb of your open right hand on your chin two times.

help

Place your right fist in your open left hand. Use your left hand to lift your right hand.

Dorothy Hoffman Levi is a writer and teacher. She lives in New York City with her three children, Heather, Ron, and Kara. Her comments on contemporary life have been published in several newspapers, including *The New York Times.* She has received a grant from the New York State Department of Education and a scholarship from *The New York Times.* This is her second children's book. She is currently completing a novel. ▪

Ethel Gold is an illustrator who lives in a suburb of New York City with an elderly Norwegian elkhound and four cats. She mostly does illustrations for children's books, although she has worked in advertising and won a New York Art Director's Club Award for a magazine cover. Ms. Gold has a grown daughter. ▪